MOUTHS AND BITS

by

Toni Webber

Illustrations by

Carole Vincer

KENILWORTH PRESS

First published in Great Britain by
Threshold Books, The Kenilworth Press Limited,
Addington, Buckingham, MK18 2JR

© The Kenilworth Press Limited 1990
Reprinted 1991, 1992, 1994, 1995, 1996, 1999, 2002, 2005

British Library Cataloguing in Publication Data
A catalogue record for this book is available from the British Library.

ISBN 1-872082-09-2

Typeset by Kenilworth Press

Printed in Great Britain by Halstan & Co Ltd.

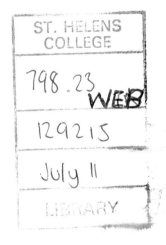

CONTENTS

Introduction

The horse's mouth is perfectly shaped for wearing a bit. At exactly the point where a metal bar can be suspended without pinching the lips, the jawbone has no teeth. Properly adjusted, the bit cannot bang against the teeth, nor can the horse grip the bit so firmly that it can ignore the wishes of its rider.

Other animals must be controlled by other means – nose-rings, perhaps, or a noose round the nose or lower jaw – but these methods often rely on inflicting pain to gain obedience.

With a horse, however, a much more delicate signalling system can be established. Depending on its style, the bit acts on different parts of the horse's mouth and combines with other aids – the voice, legs, the weight and position of the rider's body – to tell the horse to turn left or right, slow down, stop, or move sideways or backwards.

Bits have been in existence for several thousand years, and horsemen throughout equestrian history have experimented with their shape. Even today, the average saddlery shop carries a wide range of bits and most horse owners are tempted at times to experiment for themselves.

The reason for this is that every horse is as much an individual as its rider; the bit that suits one horse's mouth may not suit another's. Some horses have thick tongues, some have thin ones; some are long in the mouth, others short. And the nerve-endings in the mouth can vary in sensitivity.

The difference between your horse's mouth and the next one's may not be great, but if you understand the anatomy of the mouth as well as the temperament of your horse you are more likely to find the bit which will suit him best.

Evolution of the mouth

The horse's remote ancestor was a small fawn-like creature which lived in forests and browsed on leaves. It was called EOHIPPUS, the 'dawn horse'. Its head was more pointed than that of the modern horse and its profile more convex but, as can be seen from the diagram of its skull (*below*), the main difference between its mouth and that of its descendants was the shape of the teeth and the depth of its jaw-line.

Eohippus had forty-four teeth. The molars had low crowns and long roots, with conical cusps specially adapted for browsing on leaves in the swampy forests. The jaw-line was less heavily developed than is found in the fossil remains of later horses.

Eohippus lived 50 million years ago. Its descendants grew gradually bigger and their bodies underwent many changes as they developed into the horses we know today. The main change in their skulls, however, lies in the jaw-line, which increased in strength and size to accommodate teeth with higher crowns, as the horses moved out on to the plains and lived on grass rather than leaves.

At around the time of MESOHIPPUS (25-40 million years ago), the gap between the front and back teeth developed. This species and the nearer ancestors of the present horse – MERYCHIPPUS (15-20 million years ago) and PLIOHIPPUS (6-10 million years ago) – all show the same sequence of molars, gap, tushes and incisors that you will see if you look in the mouth of your own horse.

The true horse, EQUUS CABALLUS, appeared on earth within the last million years. It was this animal that our ancestors first tamed and fitted with a bridle and bit.

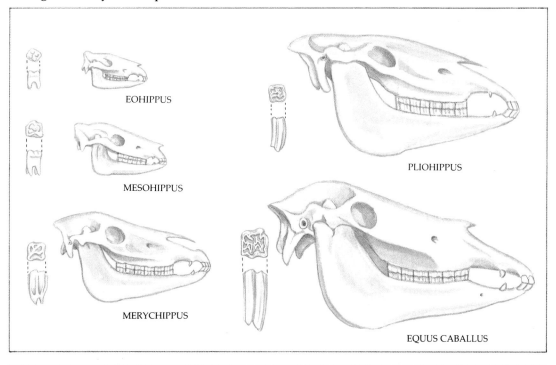

EOHIPPUS

MESOHIPPUS

MERYCHIPPUS

PLIOHIPPUS

EQUUS CABALLUS

Anatomy of the mouth

The shape of the horse's mouth shows it to be a vegetarian. The neat row of incisors at the front of the mouth, six on both upper and lower jaws, are designed to tear at growing grass. In fact, it is the horse's method of grazing – taking the grass in an abrupt sideways motion, often ripping out the grass by the roots – which makes it an uneconomical feeder.

Behind the row of incisors are the canine teeth, or tushes, which are normally present only in male horses and usually appear when the horse is between four and five years old. The gap between the upper tushes and the upper incisors is greater than in the lower jaw. In consequence, the tushes do not meet and there is very little change in their appearance as the horse grows older.

The toothless surfaces of each jaw, and the place where the bit rests, are known as the bars. They lie more or less parallel to the chin groove.

Towards the back of the mouth, six on each side in both upper and lower jaws, are the cheek teeth, the molars. These are the teeth which prepare the food for swallowing. Constant grinding gradually wears away the surface, but the length of the exposed teeth remains roughly the same as extra bone develops beneath them. Sometimes the wear is uneven and sharp edges develop, which is why older horses in particular should have their teeth checked regularly and, if necessary, rasped.

The wolf teeth – tiny teeth which grow hard against the premolars – may be removed if they interfere with the bit. Not all horses, however, develop them and, even if they do, they may not affect the comfort of the bit.

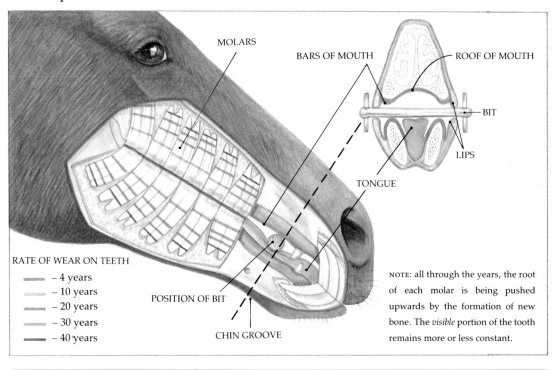

MOLARS

BARS OF MOUTH

ROOF OF MOUTH

BIT

LIPS

TONGUE

RATE OF WEAR ON TEETH

- 4 years
- 10 years
- 20 years
- 30 years
- 40 years

POSITION OF BIT

CHIN GROOVE

NOTE: all through the years, the root of each molar is being pushed upwards by the formation of new bone. The *visible* portion of the tooth remains more or less constant.

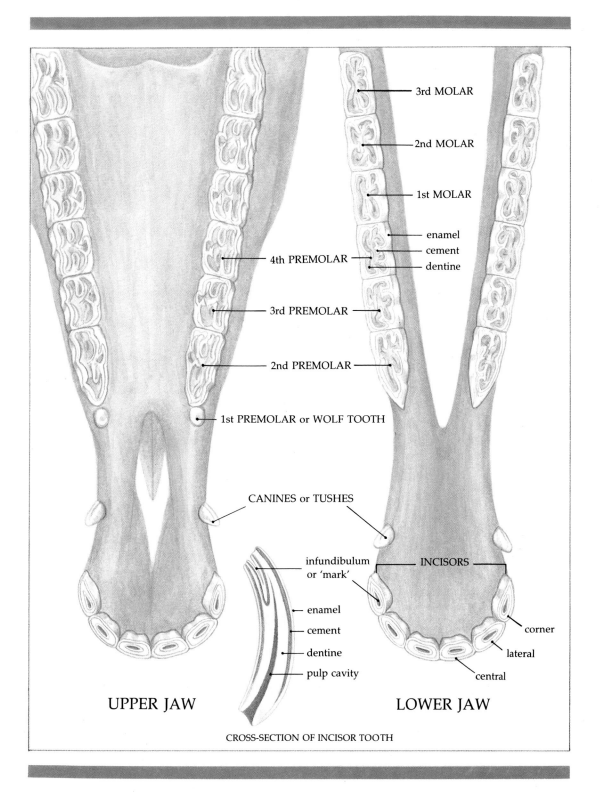

3rd MOLAR

2nd MOLAR

1st MOLAR

enamel
cement
dentine

4th PREMOLAR

3rd PREMOLAR

2nd PREMOLAR

1st PREMOLAR or WOLF TOOTH

CANINES or TUSHES

infundibulum
or 'mark'

INCISORS

enamel

cement

dentine

pulp cavity

corner

lateral

central

UPPER JAW

LOWER JAW

CROSS-SECTION OF INCISOR TOOTH

Tooth changes throughout life

Most people know that it is possible to tell the age of a horse by looking at its teeth. However, an accurate assessment is feasible only up to the age of eight. After that, the changes that occur in the teeth are more gradual, and the appearance of the teeth can be only a rough guide.

The drawings on this and the following pages show the ages at which progress in development occurs. The differences look very clear in the pictures, but with a live horse it is quite difficult to pinpoint its age correctly. Many horses object to having their mouths opened and their teeth examined, and will not keep their jaws still while you are peering at their teeth.

It is wise, therefore, not to rely only on an examination of the teeth to determine a horse's age. Always look for other indications.

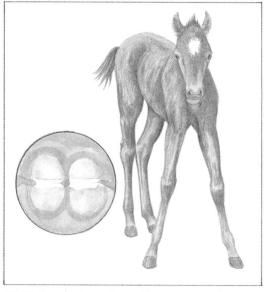

At **birth** a foal's milk teeth are covered by a thin membrane. The first teeth to erupt are the two central incisors and two or three molars.

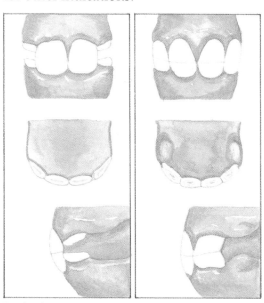

In the first **5 months** the next incisors appear but it will be two to three months later before the corner incisors begin to show through the gum.

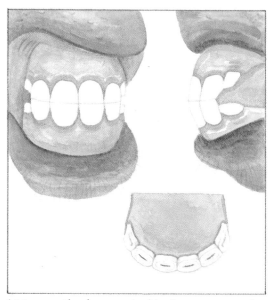

At **1 year**, the four central incisors meet and the corner incisors can be clearly seen. The yearling's first permanent molars appear.

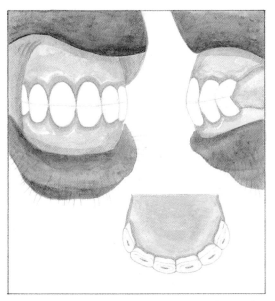

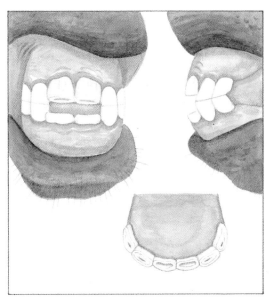

By **2 years old** all the milk teeth are through. The young horse may begin to show signs of teething as the permanent teeth start to grow.

The first permanent incisors appear at **2½ years**. The milk teeth loosen and fall out and the young horse has the gappy look of a human 6-year-old.

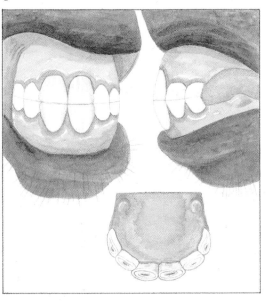

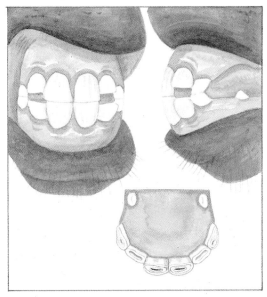

By **3 years old** the horse has two large, yellowish permanen incisors in both jaws, with white milk teeth beginning to loosen on either side.

At **3½ years** the last milk teeth are being replaced by permanent ones. In some male horses, the canine teeth or tushes on the lower jaw may appear.

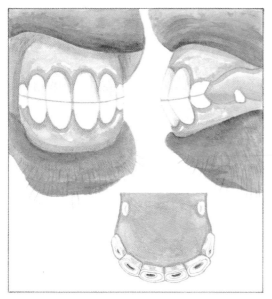

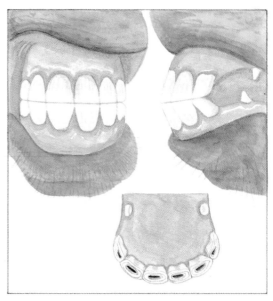

The **4-year-old** has four permanent incisors in each jaw, their yellow colour contrasting with the corner incisors, which still have to be shed.

At **5** the horse has all 12 permanent incisors. Its mouth is distinguished from the 2-year-old's by the darkness of the 'marks' on the biting surface.

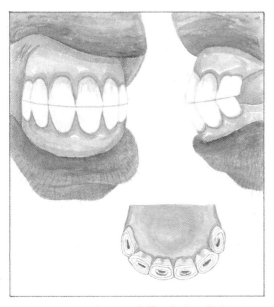

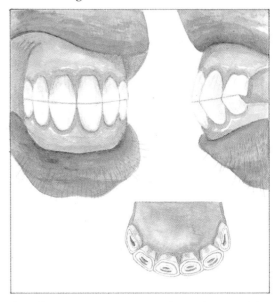

At **6** it is getting quite difficult to tell the age of the horse. The marks on the two central incisors are now smaller than the rest.

At **7** the corner incisors are the only ones left with large marks. These teeth have developed a small projection at the rear – the 7-year hook.

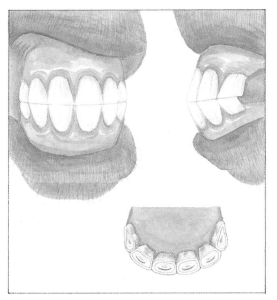

It is still possible at **8 years old** to tell the age accurately from the teeth. The marks are similar on all teeth and the 7-year-hook has disappeared.

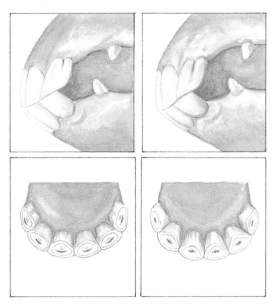

Galvayne's groove, a small furrow, appears at the top of the outer incisor at around **10 years old**. At **15** it has reached about halfway down the tooth.

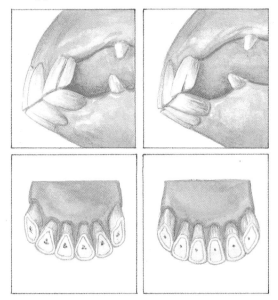

The groove reaches the biting surface at about **20** and by **25** has almost gone. As the horse ages, the teeth become yellower, longer and more sloping.

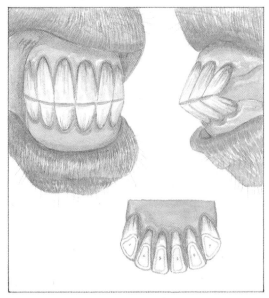

The marks on a horse aged between **25 and 30** have faded, and the biting surface is no longer oval in shape. Galvayne's groove has disappeared completely.

Care of the mouth

Treated properly, the horse is by and large a healthy creature. All good, conscientious horse owners endeavour to feed their animals on sensible, well-balanced diets, give them adequate exercise and keep a sharp eye open for any sign of illness or loss of condition.

As far as the mouth is concerned, problems are rare. A horse's teeth tend to remain in good condition throughout its life; dental caries, for example, seldom occurs, and other ailments, such as inflammation of the gums, abscesses or mouth ulcers, are not often seen in the horse.

The most common complaint is uneven wear of the cheek teeth, or molars. The molars in the upper jaw are set very slightly more widely apart than those in the lower jaw. After a while it is possible for a hook to develop on the outside edge of the upper teeth and on the inside edge of the lower ones. This can lead to difficulty in masticating and occasionally to abrasions and ulcers. Rasping, carried out by the vet, is a simple job and quickly removes the sharp points.

Always have the teeth inspected regularly and, if necessary, rasped. *Quidding*, when the horse dribbles food from its mouth, is a sign that its teeth may need attention.

Uneven wear on the incisors may be a sign that the horse is crib-biting, a habit which may develop in a stabled horse through boredom.

Physical deformitites of the mouth, such as *parrot mouth*, where the upper incisors overhang the lower, and *sow mouth*, the reverse condition, are usually hereditary and unless very severe do not affect the horse's well-being.

As a horse gets older, the molars may wear unevenly, forming sharp edges which interfere with eating and may cut the mouth. The teeth must be **rasped**.

Rasping is not painful for the horse but the tongue may get in the way. A helper can **hold the tongue** to one side or a **restraining device** may be used.

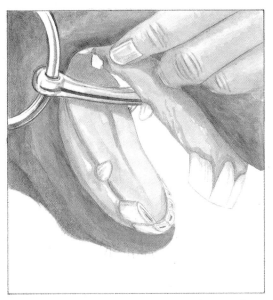

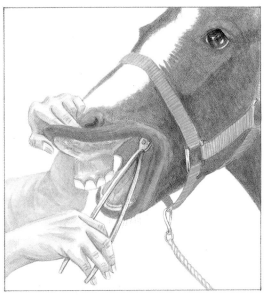

Tiny **wolf teeth** sometimes erupt close to the first of the molars or cheek teeth. If the gum is inflamed or they interfere with the bit, they must be removed.

Wolf teeth have such small roots that the teeth can be **extracted** without an anaesthtic. Just a quick pull with a pair of forceps is all that is needed.

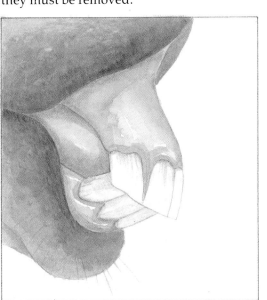

In most horses, the biting surfaces of the incisors meet evenly. If the upper jaw is longer than the lower, the horse is said to have a '**parrot mouth**'.

A much less common variation than the parrot mouth is the undershot jaw, or '**sow mouth**'. Neither deformity seems to affect the horse's feeding ability.

The tongue

The main function of the tongue is to act as a conveyor belt, moving food from the front of the mouth to the molars and from there into the gullet. Its muscles are strong and it contains salivary glands which discharge enzyme-filled fluid through tiny openings on the tongue into the mouth. The fluid helps to break down the food and starts the digestive process.

The tongue is used for licking, normally to obtain essential minerals – from bare earth, salt blocks, etc. It is not used for drinking – a horse does not lap like a dog or cat but draws water up through the lips – although its muscular action helps to convey the water to the gullet. Nor is it used for grooming in the way a cat will.

A mare, however, will use her tongue on her new-born foal, licking and nudging it in the first minutes after

By **licking** and nudging her newborn foal, a mare encourages it to struggle to its feet, and helps to establish the bond between them.

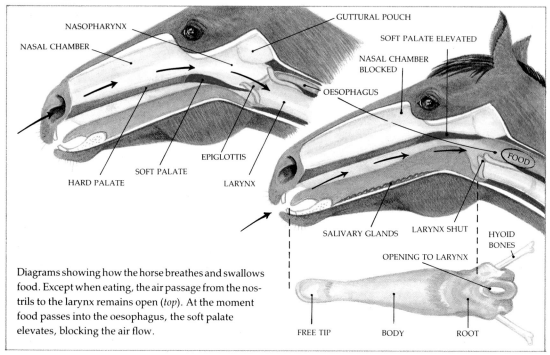

Diagrams showing how the horse breathes and swallows food. Except when eating, the air passage from the nostrils to the larynx remains open (*top*). At the moment food passes into the oesophagus, the soft palate elevates, blocking the air flow.

NASOPHARYNX

NASAL CHAMBER

GUTTURAL POUCH

SOFT PALATE ELEVATED

NASAL CHAMBER BLOCKED

OESOPHAGUS

EPIGLOTTIS

HARD PALATE

SOFT PALATE

LARYNX

FOOD

SALIVARY GLANDS

LARYNX SHUT

HYOID BONES

OPENING TO LARYNX

FREE TIP

BODY

ROOT

birth to encourage it to get to its feet. And a horse with a cut or wound may 'worry' the place with its tongue.

'Swallowing the tongue' is a phrase used to describe something that can occur when a horse is moving fast, most commonly on a racecourse. The horse suddenly checks its stride, makes a gurgling noise in the throat and then continues as though nothing had happened.

At one time, it was believed that the horse really had swallowed its tongue, but we now know that the problem is connected with the soft palate, the membrane at the back of the throat which directs air into the larynx. A sudden lack of tension in the soft palate shuts off the air flow, causing the horse to gasp and stop galloping. The horse recovers quickly but by then will have lost its position in the race.

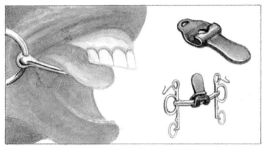

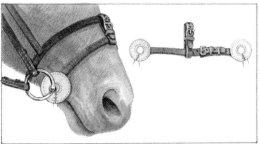

Sometimes a horse gets its **tongue over the bit**; the rider then has no control. A rubber **tongue port** (*top*) and **tongue strap** (*bottom*) offer solutions.

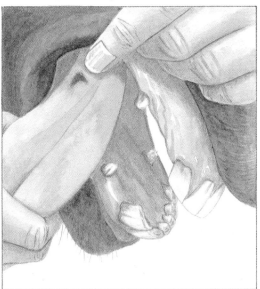

Sore **abrasions** on the tongue can be caused by harsh use of a severe bit, or by sharp edges on the bit or teeth. Rasp the teeth or change the bit.

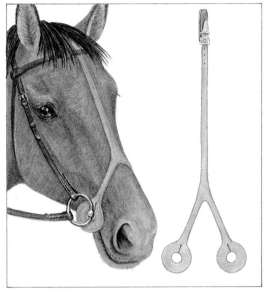

The **Australian cheeker** helps to prevent a horse from getting its tongue over the bit. It fastens to the headband and holds the bit high in the mouth.

Condition of the mouth

The colour of the gums and palate is a good indication of the general health of the horse, and it is sensible to examine the mouth from time to time, particularly if your horse appears to be under the weather.

Healthy gums are a fine pink colour, but fade to off-white if the horse is anaemic or in shock. Very sickly-looking, pallid gums could also mean an internal haemorrhage, but in this case there would be other symptoms. In a horse suffering from jaundice – most commonly seen in new-born foals – the membranes take on a distinctly yellow hue.

Lumps under the jaw, swelling of the palate or blood-flecked saliva are all signs of something amiss. Generally, you should suspect the teeth first and call in the vet if you cannot immediately find the cause.

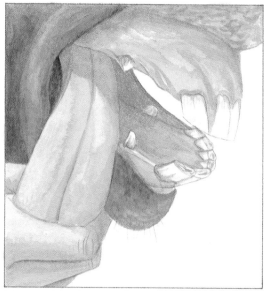

To examine the mouth, grasp the tongue firmly and pull it to one side, out of the way. This is a **healthy** mouth, as shown by the pink colour of the gums.

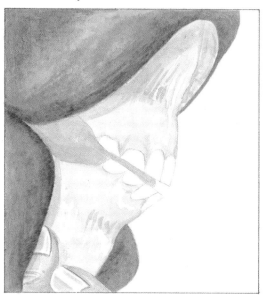

A horse which is **anaemic** loses most of the pinkness from the membranes of the mouth, leaving them a pale, whitish colour as shown here.

Jaundice is a symptom of a number of blood or liver disorders, and is quite common in foals. It is shown by a distinct yellowing of the membranes.

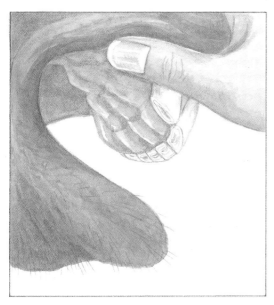

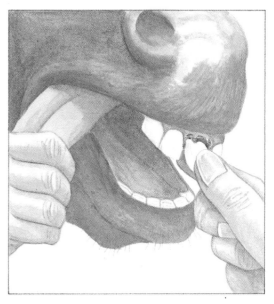

Lampas is a hard swelling of the membrane lining the hard palate behind the upper incisors. The ridge may reach tooth depth but is not serious.

Milk teeth should loosen and fall out of their own accord as the permanent teeth push their way up from below. Sometimes, they may need a little help.

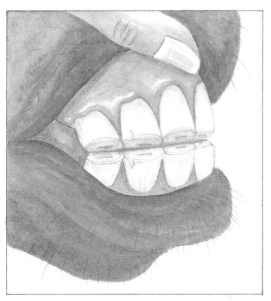

Unnatural wear on the incisors is a sign of **crib-biting**. This vice, in which the horse swallows air whilst gripping the manger or stable door, may affect the horse's wind.

If a horse develops a hard swelling or discharging wound on the lower jaw, the cause could be an **impacted tooth** or, rarely, some form of dental disease.

Bits

A 'snaffle mouth' is widely prized; it is a good point to advertise when selling a horse, and in the Pony Club a snaffle is the only bit permitted in many competitions.

The reason is that the snaffle is generally a fairly mild bit, although there are variations which are severe. A horse which goes well in a snaffle is likely to be fairly well mannered and responsive to its rider.

But horses are highly individual, and some may put up a better performance in a bit with a totally different action from a snaffle. The Pelham, for example, combines the actions of curb and snaffle bits with a single mouthpiece and is best used with two reins.

The double bridle uses both curb and snaffle together but, because it has two mouthpieces, should be used only by experienced riders.

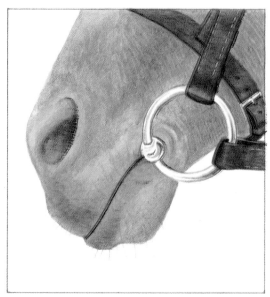

A snaffle bit **correctly fitted** should hang so that the corners of the mouth are slightly wrinkled and the horse appears to be smiling.

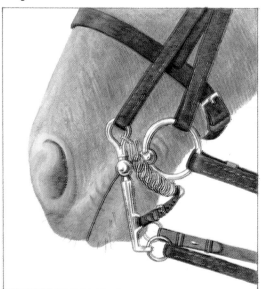

A **double bridle** is worn with the snaffle or bradoon bit above the curb. The curb should always be fitted with a curb chain and lip strap.

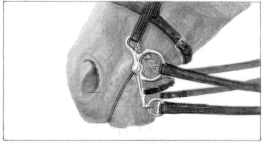

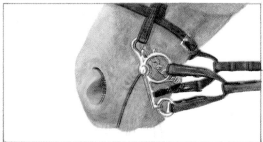

When two reins are used (*top*), the **Pelham** bit gives the rider more subtle control than the same bit with **roundings** and a single rein (*bottom*).

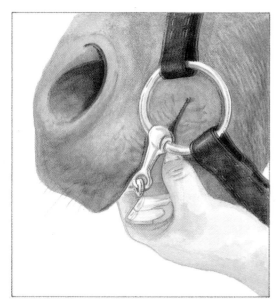

Inserting your **thumb** into the corner of the horse's mouth will cause it to open. The bit can then be slipped into position in one easy movement.

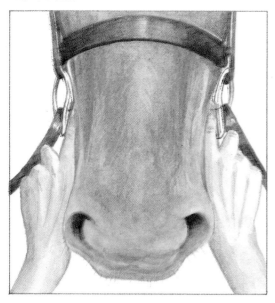

Check that the **width** of the bit is just right by placing your index fingers between the mouth and the bit rings. The fingers should fit snugly.

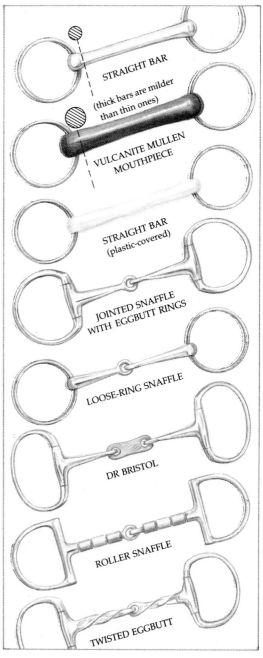

STRAIGHT BAR
(thick bars are milder than thin ones)

VULCANITE MULLEN MOUTHPIECE

STRAIGHT BAR
(plastic-covered)

JOINTED SNAFFLE WITH EGGBUTT RINGS

LOOSE-RING SNAFFLE

DR BRISTOL

ROLLER SNAFFLE

TWISTED EGGBUTT

Range of bits, from very mild (*top*) to severe (*bottom*). The roller snaffle encourages the horse to play with the bit. Eggbutts prevent the bit from pinching the lips.

Action of the bit

When pressure is applied via the hands and reins to the bit, the pressure is transferred to the horse in a number of ways, depending on the type of bit being used.

The straight bar acts simply on the bars of the mouth. If the mouthpiece is jointed in the middle, it has a nutcracker effect on the tongue and squeezes the corners of the mouth.

A curb bit applies leverage to the poll – the longer the shanks, the greater the leverage. A curb chain, if fitted, presses on the chin groove.

The style of the mouthpiece is a good guide to the mildness or severity of the bit. Thick, straight mouthpieces are very mild. If the mouthpiece is convex (mullen) it leaves plenty of room for the tongue. One with a high bulge, or port, in the centre of the mouthpiece, acts on the roof of the mouth.

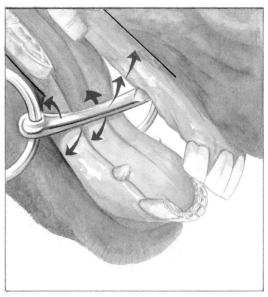

A **straight-bar** mouthpiece acts on the tongue and the bars of the mouth in the directions indicated. Its drawback is that the horse may lean on the bit.

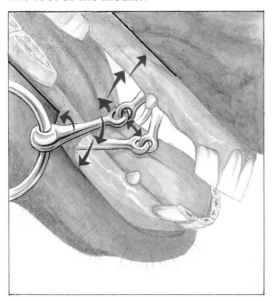

A **joint** in the middle of the mouthpiece adds a nutcracker effect to the action of the bit. This acts on the tongue and on the corners of the mouth.

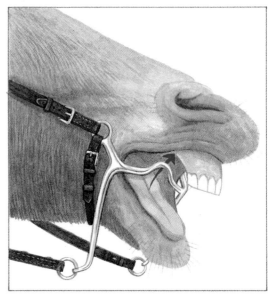

The **curb** bit depends on leverage, so that pressure is transferred from shank to poll. In this Western bit, the high port also acts on the roof of the mouth.

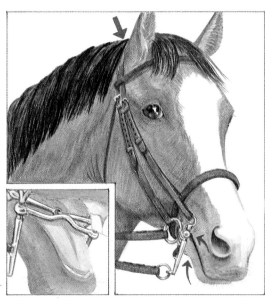

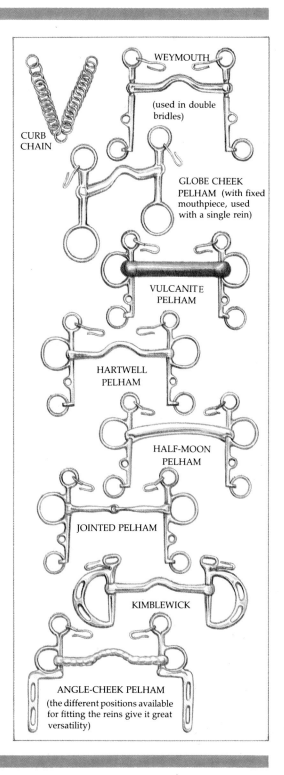

CURB
CHAIN

WEYMOUTH

(used in double bridles)

GLOBE CHEEK PELHAM (with fixed mouthpiece, used with a single rein)

The **double bridle** combines the action of curb and snaffle, applying pressure to the poll and chin groove as well as to the bars of the mouth and the tongue.

VULCANITE PELHAM

HARTWELL PELHAM

HALF-MOON PELHAM

JOINTED PELHAM

KIMBLEWICK

The **gag snaffle** is effective with some horses, acting on the poll and the corners of the mouth. Its object is to raise the head and encourage flexion.

ANGLE-CHEEK PELHAM
(the different positions available for fitting the reins give it great versatility)

Problems with bitting

Finding the right bit for your horse is not easy. If you think you have a problem, you should always consult an expert, preferably one who can watch you in a school or accompany you on a ride. If you can, try borrowing a different bit before going to the expense of buying one.

A horse may try to evade the bit, perhaps by opening its mouth, raising its head or by setting or crossing its jaw. If you are satisfied that it is not your riding which causes it to act this way, you should examine both bridle and bit. A drop noseband or martingale could be one solution; alternatively, try a complete change of bit.

If the corners of the mouth split or show raw patches, check that the bit is not too narrow or too wide and make certain that there are no sharp edges. Bit guards may help; as may a thicker mouthpiece.

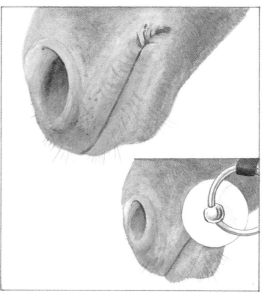

If the corners of a horse's mouth **split** easily, check that the bit fits. Chafing can be minimised by fitting rubber **bit guards** to the snaffle.

The **Kimblewick** is a popular bit for use on a snaffle-mouthed horse when greater control is needed. It lowers the head by exerting strong pressure on the poll.

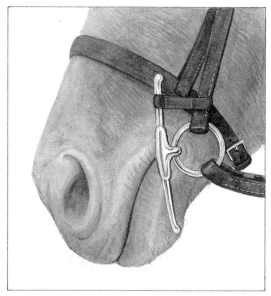

The **cheek** snaffle, or **Fulmer** snaffle, fitted with cheek retainers to keep the cheeks in place, helps to control the sideways movement of the head.

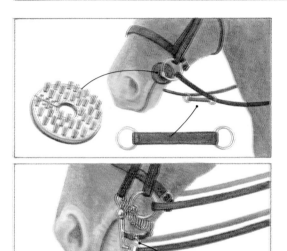

Brush pricker for horses which hang to one side; **Irish martingale** for keeping the reins in line with the mouth; **leather curb 'chain'** to prevent chafing.

A horse may evade the action of the bit by opening its mouth and setting its jaw. If so, try using a **drop noseband**, which should not be fitted too low.

If a horse **shakes** its head when being ridden, suspect an ill-fitting bridle. A browband that is too tight is a more likely culprit than a sore mouth.

Another way of evading the bit: the horse raises its head and opens its mouth. A **standing martingale** and **flash noseband** could provide the answer.

The bitless bridle

There are some horses which never learn to go well in any kind of bit. For these horses, the bitless bridle is a solution, although because of its action it should be used only by experienced riders.

All bitless bridles act on the horse's nose, using a curb-like leverage to apply pressure both to the poll and to the sensitive area above the horse's nostrils. It is a mistake to think that because it has no mouthpiece it must be very mild. Harshly used, it can cause a horse great discomfort.

There are two bitless bridles in common use, the German and English hackamores. Both apply additional pressure to the jaw. The South American bosal, on the other hand, is used mainly for breaking purposes. It acts on the nose and the weight of the rawhide knot helps to train the horse in neck-reining.

The **English hackamore** has a metal shank and a broad, padded noseband, which presses on the nose. The leather curb 'chain' acts on the chin groove.

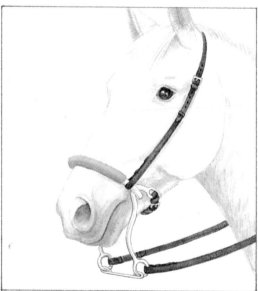

The **German hackamore** is similar to the English type in its use and purpose. Bitless bridles are useful if a horse will not accept a conventional bit.

In the **South American bosal**, the rawhide knot acts as a counterweight to keep the nosepiece in position. It also swings to encourage neck-reining.